The
Shark
and the
Shipwreck

Written by Celia Warren

Illustrated by Jan Smith

Rigby

Two little skeletons,
Skid and Skip,
swim along to
the wreck of a ship.
Skid has a patch
and a scarf on his head,
Skip has a big
black hat instead.

2

Skid clicks a latch
and gives it a thump.
He flicks up the hatch
and down they jump.
It's dark in the hold
of the old shipwreck.
They don't catch sight
of a shark on the deck.

In the light of the lamp
they see gold bars,
scarlet stones
and charms in jars,
sparkling dishes,
treasures from afar,
a velvet carpet
as bright as a star.

Skip picks up
some golden charms.
It's hard to hold them
all in his arms.

Skid spots a harp
and tries to snatch it.
His big sharp elbow
starts to scratch it.
He plucks a string
and begins to sing.
Skip cries, "Stop!
Don't harm that thing!

Put everything
on the deck in a pile.
We'll collect it all
in a little while."
Skid and Skip
empty the hold.
Up on the deck
go the charms and the gold.

The hungry shark
swims around the wreck.
She swallows the treasure
dumped on the deck.
A noise from below
makes her jump in fright.
She swims off quickly
into the night.

Arm in arm,
the skeletons skip.
They have had
a marvelous trip.

But up on deck,
they get a shock.
Where, oh where,
is their treasure stock?

"Help!" cries Skip.
"Behind you – a shark!"
The skeletons cling
together in the dark.
But the shark looks ill
from her lumpy snack.
The skeletons know
she will not attack.

Pardon me
for my silly trick.
I swallowed your treasure
and now I feel sick.
I swallowed it all,
every bar, every dish.
But from now on
I will stick to fish!